1479
blue 952

ALD JACKSON SCHOOL
MARSH LANE
GAYWOOD, KING'S LYNN
PE30 3AE
Tel: (01553) 672779/674281
Fax: (01553) 670344

W0028565

games people play!

Japan

Philip Brooks

CHILDREN'S PRESS®
A Division of Grolier Publishing
New York • London • Hong Kong • Sydney
Danbury, Connecticut

Editorial Staff

Project Editor: Mark Friedman
Photo Research: Feldman & Associates
Fact Checker: Dana Burnell
Intern: Amy Vivio

Design Staff

Design and Electronic Composition:
   TJS Design
Maps: TJS Design
Cover Art and Icons: Susan Kwas
Activity Page Art: MacArt Design

Library of Congress Cataloging-in-Publication Data

Brooks, Philip, 1963–
  Japan / by Philip Brooks.
    p.   cm.—(Games people play)
  Includes index.
  ISBN 0-516-04438-9
  1. Japan—Juvenile literature. I. Title. II. Series.

DS805.B684 1995   95-1791
952—dc20   CIP
                                                  AC

High-school track athletes show that teamwork is the key to most Japanese sports.

©1995 by Children's Press®, Inc.
All rights reserved. Published simultaneously in Canada.
Printed in the United States of America
1 2 3 4 5 6 7 8 9 10 R 04 03 02 01 00 99 98 97 96 95

Table of Contents

4	Japan: Hard Work and Play
8	Japan at a Glance
10	The National Pastime
20	The Martial Arts: Bushido
28	The Great American Game in Japan
36	Golf and Other Western Sports
46	Games Kids Play
52	Flying Carp and Magic Cranes
60	Glossary
62	Index

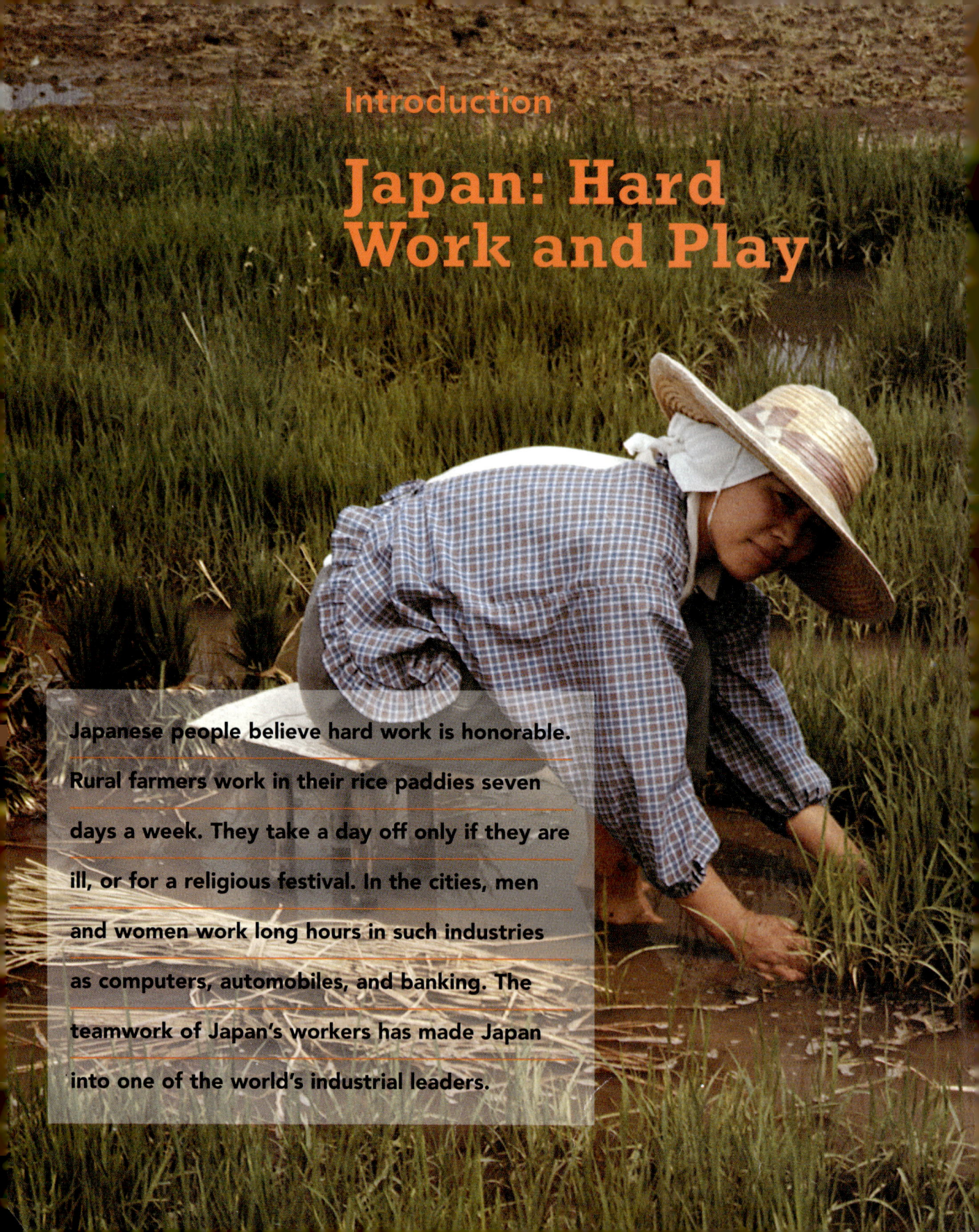

Introduction

Japan: Hard Work and Play

Japanese people believe hard work is honorable. Rural farmers work in their rice paddies seven days a week. They take a day off only if they are ill, or for a religious festival. In the cities, men and women work long hours in such industries as computers, automobiles, and banking. The teamwork of Japan's workers has made Japan into one of the world's industrial leaders.

Japanese schoolchildren work hard in school, and sometimes they study just as hard at home.

Japanese parents push their children to succeed with the same intensity. Many parents disapprove of teachers allowing young children to simply "play." Some Japanese believe that unstructured play is a waste of time. Many parents hire private tutors to work with their children after school—or even on Saturdays and Sundays!

In Japan, bullet trains link tranquil farming villages to crowded cities such as Tokyo and Osaka.

A price has been paid, however, for all this hard work and success. Many Japanese people are overworked. Some do not spend enough time with their families. Some are so driven to succeed that they endanger their health by working very long hours, or by smoking cigarettes and drinking alcohol.

In recent years, Japanese people have begun striving for a balance between work and play. Japan has a rich and ancient tradition of festivals, games, and sports. People still take time to participate in centuries-old traditional sports, such as the martial arts of *karate* and *judo*. And the long-lasting tradition of *sumo* wrestling is a national passion. What's more, Western sports such as baseball, golf, football, and basketball have become wildly popular in Japan.

Many people in the United States think of sports as a way to relax and just have fun. Recently, Japanese companies have begun demanding fewer hours from their employees. With time to relax, Tokyo business people now take the time for a round of golf, or they will spend a weekend skiing in the mountains. But they treat sports and games with strict attention to Japanese style and tradition. Teamwork, rigorous physical training, and intense mental concentration remain the foundation of all activities in Japan, especially sports.

Japanese office workers take time out of their busy day for exercise.

Japan at a Glance

The Land
Japan consists of a series of islands that form a 1,500-mile arc in the Pacific Ocean. The four main islands of Japan are Hokkaido, Honshu, Shikoku, and Kyushu. Japan's thriving capital, Tokyo, is located on Honshu's eastern coast.

The People
More than 8.2 million people live in Tokyo, one of the most densely populated spots in the world. More than 123 million people live in Japan as a whole. Their language is Japanese, and they practice the Buddhist, Shinto, and Christian religions.

Government
The Japanese system of government is called a "constitutional monarchy." They have an emperor, but his position is almost entirely ceremonial; he plays no active role in governing the country. The real business of government takes place in the Parliament.

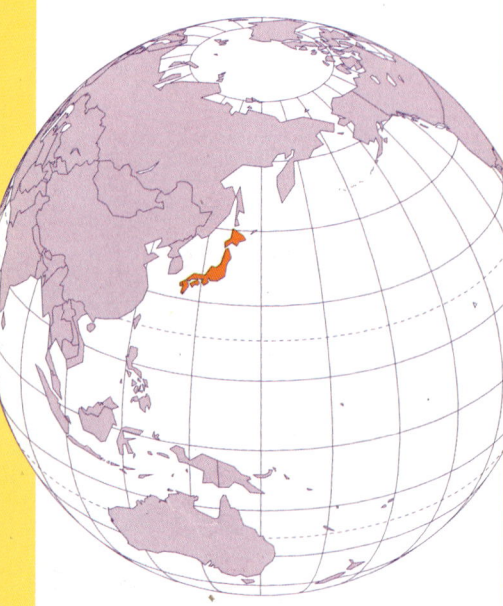

History
Japan's written history begins in A.D. 500. From the 1100s through much of the 1800s, power lay with feudal lords and warriors called *shoguns*. In 1868, Mutshuhito became emperor of Japan, ending shogun domination. Under Mutshuhito, Japan began to trade with the West, and heavy industries began growing in Japan. In World War II (1939-45), Japan sided with Germany and Italy, and was defeated by the United States and its allies. After the war ended, the United States helped create a democratic system of government in Japan. Today, Japan is one of the world's richest and most technologically advanced nations. Japan and the United States are strong allies, despite occasional disagreements concerning trade.

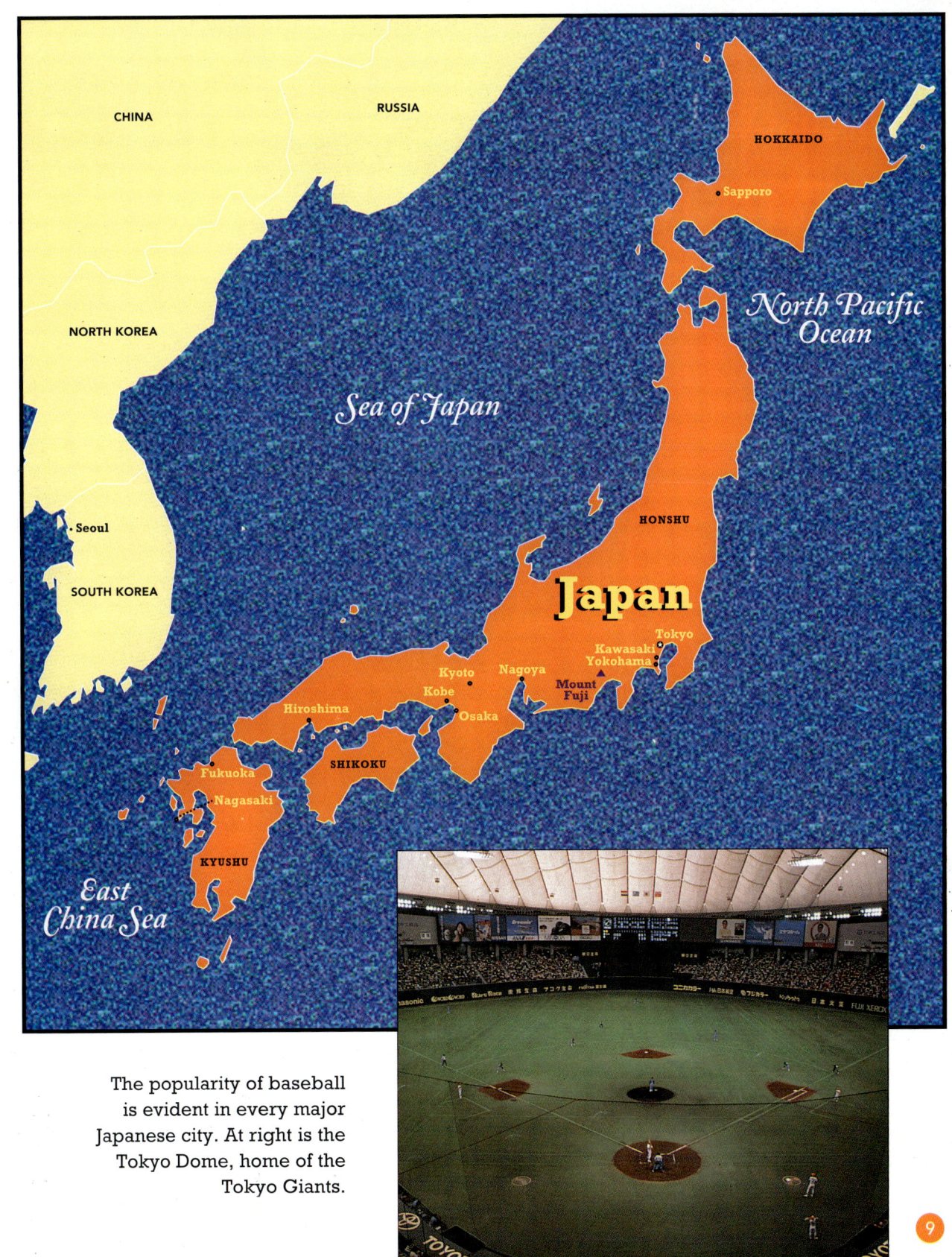

The popularity of baseball is evident in every major Japanese city. At right is the Tokyo Dome, home of the Tokyo Giants.

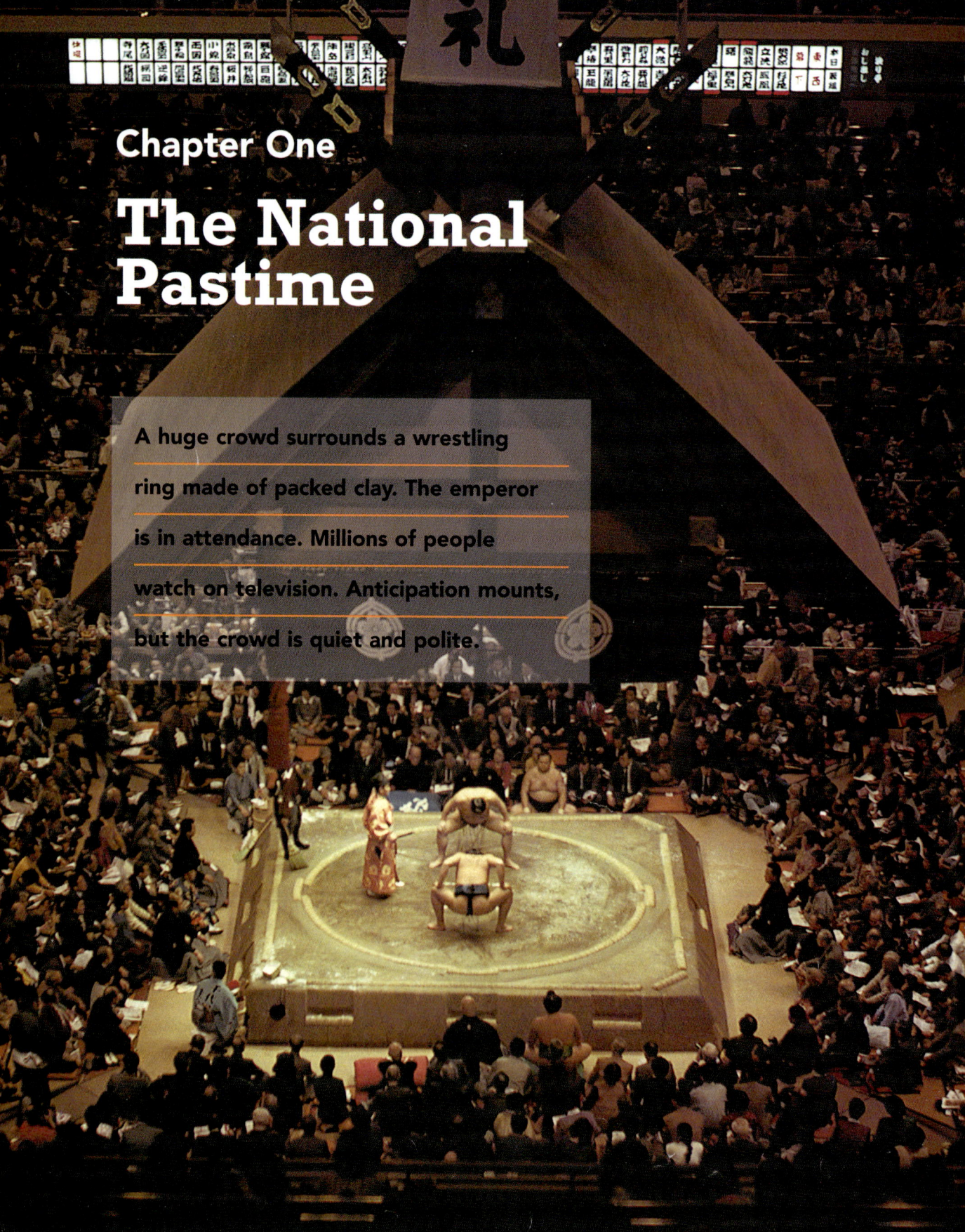

Chapter One

The National Pastime

A huge crowd surrounds a wrestling ring made of packed clay. The emperor is in attendance. Millions of people watch on television. Anticipation mounts, but the crowd is quiet and polite.

Six times a year, fifteen-day competitions called *basho* are held to determine who is *yokozuna* (grand champion) of Japanese **sumo wrestling**. The most important of these basho awards is the Emperor's Cup. This sumo tournament carries as much importance in Japan as the Super Bowl does in the United States.

Sumo wrestlers enter the ring dressed in traditional, colorful costumes.

The electricity in the sumo ring grows. At last, the *yokozuna dohyoiri* (the "ring entrance of grand champions") begins. A parade of huge wrestlers enters the arena. They wear brightly colored robes and elaborate hairstyles tied in topknots. The wrestlers line up around the ring and face the crowd. Each wrestler weighs more than three hundred pounds, and many top four hundred pounds! Then, the first two wrestlers remove their robes and enter the ring wearing nothing more than black loincloths.

yokozuna dohyoiri

ring entrance of grand champions

After entering the ring, the giant wrestlers glower, huff, and puff to strike fear in one another. They clap their hands to summon the attention of divine Shinto spirits, and they stamp their feet to chase away evil spirits. They bow and slap the ground, then toss handfuls of salt over their shoulders to purify themselves and the ring. They even drink special purifying water called *chikane-mizu*.

Before sumo wrestlers attack each other, they throw salt (right) and stomp around the ring (above).

With the *gyoj* (far left) watching closely, the wrestler on the left comes close to falling outside the ring. If he does, he will lose the match.

After four minutes of this stamping, bowing, slapping, and puffing, the match begins. The two huge men run forward and crash into one another like bull elephants. There are two ways to defeat an opponent. You can wrestle him outside the 4.55-meter ring. Or, you can force any part of his body (other than the soles of his feet) to touch the ground inside the ring.

If neither man manages to win quickly, the referee separates the wrestlers. The referee is called a *gyoj*. He wears a fourteenth-century-style embroidered jacket and a tall, black hat. He carries an iron fan called a *gumabi*. This type of fan was once carried by ancient warriors. After several more minutes of ritual stamping and clapping, the referee allows the match to begin again.

referee of sumo match

Sumo wrestling is the most Japanese of all sports. It exists in no other country. Sumo-style matches are described in religious texts from as early as A.D. 800. Legend has it that the first sumo match took place between two gods. The winner ruled Japan.

According to the Shinto religion, there are divine spirits, *kami*, who watch over and govern much of human activity. Sumo matches took place in the courtyards of Shinto shrines during planting and harvesting time to entertain these divine spirits. It was believed that happy spirits might help farmers' crops.

The ancient sport of sumo wrestling dates back to A.D. 800. The wrestlers pictured at right are from the 1700s.

Sumo wrestlers endure endless hours of practice.

Sumo has gradually become a sport, rather than a religious practice. But the sacred rituals performed in the sumo ring continue. The Japanese love ritual and attention to detail. In Japanese culture, every aspect of life becomes an art form. And sport is no exception. Sumo fans love the ceremonial stomping that comes before a match as much as the battle itself.

To foreigners, sumo wrestlers may appear to be giant blobs of blubber, but they are actually highly trained and respected athletes. Nearly every boy in Japan dreams of putting on a *mawashi* (the sumo wrestler's loincloth) and entering the ring to the cheers of thousands. But before a young man can become a *sumotori* (a professional wrestler), he must undergo years of training, as well as time as an apprentice.

sumotori

professional sumo wrestler

Training to Become a Sumotori

Most apprentice sumo wrestlers are recruited as teenagers. They must work very hard to move up to the level of *sumotori,* or professional. During their training they live in stables called *heya.* They are not allowed to marry, and they receive only room and board for their work. The stables are run by an *oyakata* (which means "boss"), who is a retired champion. Oyakatas are strict. Apprentices learn humility by acting as servants to the older, more experienced sumotori. The young wrestlers must prepare and serve the sumotoris' meals, and they must style and maintain their elaborate hairstyles. They also sweep and clean the heya every day. Apprentices improve their concentration and discipline through meditation training. They endure all of this mental training in addition to the same weight lifting, *teppo* pounding, sparring, and heavy eating done by the sumotori.

Even after they reach the sumotori level, wrestlers continue heavy training. They lift weights every day, and they do countless squats with heavy barbells on their shoulders. This improves their ability to shove opponents out of the ring. They lunge at a device called a *teppo.* A teppo is a wooden pole used much like a punching bag is used by a boxer. No actual punching is allowed in sumo, but wrestlers use their forearms to deliver blows to the head and shoulders—a technique called *tsuppari.* A wrestler builds hands and forearms of stone by bashing the teppo for countless hours.

A class of young sumo wrestlers

16

Japanese children grow up dreaming of becoming an *ozeki* (champion) of the sumo ring.

When they're not training, wrestlers can most often be found eating. They consume countless bowls of *chanko-nabe* ("wrestler's stew") along with pounds of boiled rice. Wrestlers wash all this food down with huge quantities of fattening beer and *sake*. Beneath those layers of blubber, a sumo wrestler's muscles are huge, too! Bulk, strength, and quickness are what make a wrestler into an *ozeki*, or champion.

ozeki

champion

There are seven hundred sumotoris in Japan. Wrestlers' careers tend to be short and difficult. Their enormous weight puts a terrible strain on their bodies. They must deal with the constant pain of pulled muscles, strained ligaments, and sprains. The vast majority retire before age thirty. Then, they face years of dieting in order to pursue another line of work.

Chad Rowan is a 490-pound, Hawaiian-born sumo wrestler called "Akebono" in Japan. On January 25, 1993, Akebono became the first foreign sumo wrestler ever promoted to the ultimate rank of *yokozuna*.

Chapter Two

The Martial Arts: *Bushido*

In medieval times, men called *samurai* engaged in terrible, bloody battles. Samurai were more than soldiers—they were warriors who lived by a strict code of honor. A samurai was willing to die to protect his employer's territory and wealth. These samurai warriors invented the martial arts.

In medieval times, the purpose of the **martial arts** was to kill another man in hand-to-hand combat. But the martial arts also teach spiritual lessons. They train the mind and teach a person to respect opponents, oneself, and the world. The samurai called this code of honor *bushido*, meaning "the way of the warrior." To become a samurai, a warrior had to learn seven martial arts:

1. Military strategy
2. Use of Western firearms
3. Mastery of the bow and arrow
4. Use of the sword
5. Judo
6. Horsemanship
7. Use of the spear

(Samurai should not be confused with "ninjas," with whom Americans have become familiar through movies and television. *Ninja* is the art of stealth and was practiced by spies and assassins.)

Yabusame is an ancient martial art that involves shooting an arrow at a target while riding a horse (opposite page). The man below is dressed in traditional Yabusame costume.

Today, the samurai are gone. Martial arts are no longer practiced for the purpose of fighting wars. They have become sports. In each of the martial arts, a system of colored belts marks a student's progress. Each of the arts has its own requirements. Generally, a black belt indicates high achievement. All martial arts emphasize *kata,* or "form." The martial arts teach very specific ways of moving, standing, and executing tasks.

Martial arts experts, if they are true to bushido, would never be bullies. When a person is trained in the martial arts, he or she is not simply taught ways to kick or punch an opponent. Students of the martial arts are taught how to think and feel about themselves and the people and things around them.

Karate is the oldest of the Japanese martial arts. Karate originated in ancient China and was introduced in Japan during the 1600s. During this time, on what are now the islands of Okinawa, citizens were forbidden to carry weapons. These were dangerous times, and islanders wanted to be able to defend themselves. So they learned the art of karate.

Karate means "empty hand." One learns to attack the most vulnerable points of an opponent's body using kicks and jabs. In demonstrations of karate, people usually chop through a wooden board with their bare hand, or kick a cement block in half. Karate is the most aggressive and destructive of the martial arts.

Young and old, Japanese have learned the art of *karate* for centuries.

Japan's Hidehiko Yoshida celebrates winning a 1992 Olympic gold medal in *judo*.

Judo is a sport with rules similar to wrestling. It involves grabbing and throwing an opponent. Judo has a system of scoring. The winner of a judo match is the first to throw an opponent to the mat, to lift an opponent over his or her shoulders, or to pin an opponent to the mat.

After Japan's defeat in World War II, American forces occupied the country. Judo was banned by the Americans because they thought it glorified fighting and war. In the 1950s, judo returned and became more popular than ever. In 1964, it became an Olympic sport. The Summer Olympic Games were held in Tokyo that year. Many Japanese were upset when a Dutchman won the first gold medal in judo. But the Japanese have gone on to win their share of medals.

Akido, like judo, developed out of an older form of martial arts called **jujitsu.** Akido relies more on skill than strength. It teaches flexibility and graceful movement as a means to avoid attackers. But it also teaches how to apply painful holds to another person.

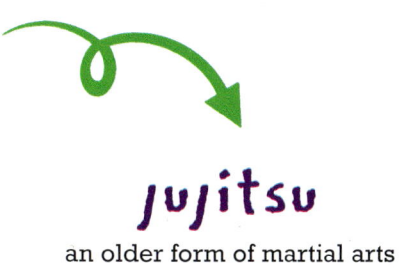

jujitsu
an older form of martial arts

Judo combatants

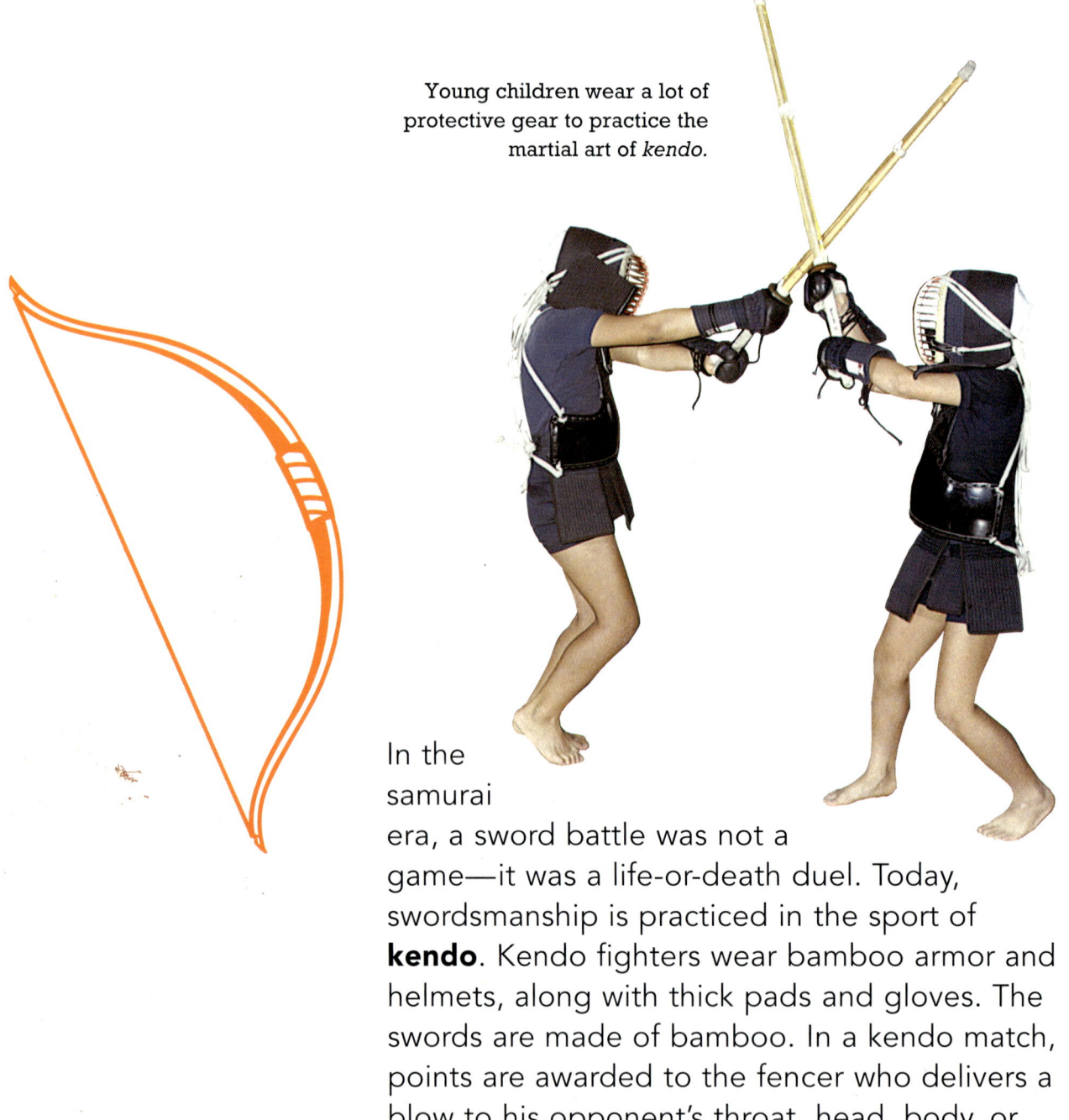

Young children wear a lot of protective gear to practice the martial art of *kendo.*

In the samurai era, a sword battle was not a game—it was a life-or-death duel. Today, swordsmanship is practiced in the sport of **kendo**. Kendo fighters wear bamboo armor and helmets, along with thick pads and gloves. The swords are made of bamboo. In a kendo match, points are awarded to the fencer who delivers a blow to his opponent's throat, head, body, or hand. The first to get two points wins.

Kyudo is a Japanese form of archery. Opponents in a match shoot arrows at a target. Originally, samurai hunted and fished with kyudo techniques; later, they used kyudo in battle. Once Western guns were introduced in Japan, archery became more an exhibition of skill than a means of killing enemy soldiers.

Kyudo archers use very long bamboo bows and arrows with bamboo shafts. Their bowstrings are made of twisted hemp, coated with resin. They wear special three-finger gloves called *yugake* to protect their hands. Kyudo trains the mind as much as the body. Archers learn not to "aim" their arrow at a target. Instead, they focus their thoughts on the target and try to "become" the arrow.

The martial arts, even in the days of the samurai, never taught followers to love battle or war. In fact, the opposite is true. Today, judo, karate, akido, kendo, and kyudo help train the bodies and minds of millions of people throughout the world. The martial arts strive to teach inner strength and harmony. They promote bushido—self-discipline and respect for others.

The martial art of *kyudo* dates back to the days before guns, when warriors used bows and arrows.

Chapter Three
The Great American Game in Japan

"Purei buro!" shouts the umpire. It sounds a little like "play ball!" And the game surely looks like American baseball. The field is exactly the same. Nine men play on a side. There are nine innings per game, and three strikes means you're out.

Some Japanese teams wear uniforms similar to those worn by American major leaguers. The Yomiuri Giants, for example, wear orange and black uniforms much like those of the San Francisco Giants. But, as American player Reggie Smith once said, "It looks like baseball, but it's something else entirely."

Before baseball arrived in the 1800s, Japan had no tradition of team sports. This is surprising, considering that Japanese society is extremely team oriented. Japanese baseball adheres to the warrior ethic called *bushido*. Ballplayers (like traditional Japanese warriors) listen to their elders, work diligently for the good of the team, and conform to the wishes of those in charge. Complainers and slackers are not tolerated. An old Japanese saying applies: "The nail that sticks up will be hammered down."

In keeping with bushido, players are extremely polite. They are forbidden to argue with an umpire. Before every game, opposing teams line up and bow to one another, and then to the umpires. Bowing to another person shows respect.

bushido

code of honor used by ancient samurai warriors

Japanese Little League teams bow to each other and to the umpires before a game begins.

On a recent tour of Japan by the Baltimore Orioles, Japanese people were astounded by star shortstop Cal Ripken, Jr. He told Japanese reporters that he had developed his own way of playing ball when he was a kid, and he had never listened to coaches who tried to change him. The Japanese would consider such a player arrogant, stubborn, and selfish. He would be criticized in the press and booed by the fans.

In Japanese baseball, training is almost a religion. Players in the United States participate in spring training for about six weeks before the season begins. Things are different in Japan.

Voluntary training starts in January— *four months* before opening day! And all players are expected to "volunteer" for pre-season training. If a player were to refuse, he would be seen as selfish and lazy. He might be traded or cut from the team.

In pre-season training, players typically spend seven hours a day on a frozen field. They take hours of batting practice. They work endlessly to master carefully planned defensive and baserunning plays. Pitchers throw as many as four hundred pitches each day! Then, they take a ten-mile run. After dinner, players return to their dormitories for several more hours of strategy meetings before bedtime.

An infielder for Japan's national baseball team, which competed in the 1992 Olympics

A Japanese Little Leaguer turns a double play.

group harmony

Players are expected to maintain this devotion to rigorous training throughout the season. Batters take as many as six hundred swings daily. Pitchers throw until their arms hurt, and then throw some more. Injured players rarely miss a game. To play through pain is what a warrior must do.

This devotion to training and teamwork is part of the Japanese effort to achieve *wa*, which means "group harmony." The success and happiness of the group is the ultimate goal in Japanese society. This harmony extends beyond one's teammates. When a baseball team wins a championship in Japan, the two teams line up and shake hands. The winners *and* losers congratulate one another on a well-played contest.

Japan's greatest baseball star, Sadahara Oh, is a perfect example of the Japanese devotion to teamwork and physical training. Sadahara Oh is the "Hank Aaron" of Japan. Oh hit 868 home runs between 1959 and 1980 and remains the home-run champion of the world. (Aaron hit 744 home runs during his career and is U.S. baseball's home-run king.) When asked how he came to be such a great hitter, Oh once said, "I achieved what I did because of my coaches and my willingness to work hard." As part of his training, Oh spent hours every day swinging a samurai sword to slice at a tiny piece of paper suspended on a string. Oh signs his autograph below the word *doryoku*, meaning "effort."

Baseball is nearly as popular in Japan as it is in the United States. But how did the Japanese come to be such baseball fanatics? In 1873, an American professor named Horace Wilson taught his favorite game to his students at the University of Tokyo. The sport

Home-run king Sadahara Oh

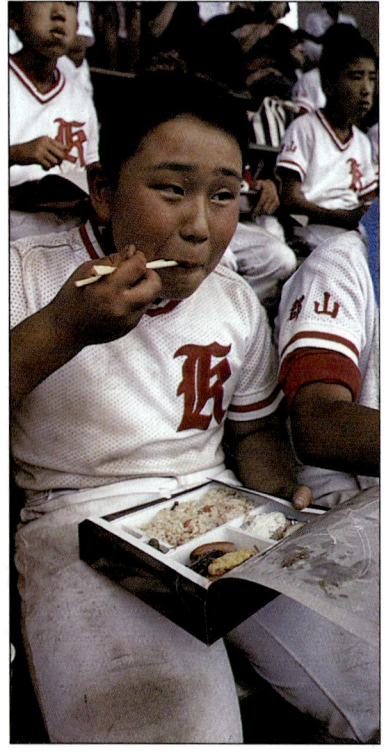

Above: A young baseball fan eats *sushi* in the stands.

Right: A cheerleader leads organized cheers at the Fukuoka Dome.

sushi

a popular way of preparing and serving fish in Japan

caught on quickly. In 1896, a college team in Tokyo routed a team of Americans, 29-4. The victory was headline news in Japan, and baseball's popularity soared throughout the nation. Soon, most colleges and high schools had teams. High-school baseball is still a hugely popular spectator sport in Japan. Many of the games are televised nationally.

In today's Japanese stadiums, if you want a hot dog or Cracker Jack, you're out of luck. Baseball stadium vendors sell noodles and *sushi*. *Sake* and glasses of whiskey are also available.

The teamwork of Japanese fans is as impressive as that of the players. Each of the twelve teams of the Central and Pacific Leagues has a professional cheerleader who leads the crowd in chants and songs. Fans of the Hiroshima Carp or Nippon Ham-Fighters sing and chant for all nine innings, no matter what the score. They are never impolite to umpires. Fans applaud effort above all else. They will cheer loudly for a great defensive play, whether it is made by the home team or the visitors. In fact, it is okay for the home team to lose, so long as it gives its best effort. The Japanese season culminates in October with the Japanese World Series. As in the United States, this is a best-of-seven-games series to determine the championship of the major leagues. It is traditional for the champions to toss their manager into the air after they have clinched the final game. Certain key players may be so honored as well!

The Babe Meets His Match

In 1934, American baseball hero Babe Ruth led a group of U.S. baseball stars on a tour of Japan. The team went undefeated. Fans flocked to see them at every stop. They were amazed by how big and strong the American players were.

But the highlight of the tour for the Japanese was not a towering shot off the Babe's mighty bat. It was the streaking fastball of an eighteen-year-old Japanese high school student. His name was **Eiji Sawamura**. Eiji stunned the Americans when he struck out Charlie Gehringer, Babe Ruth, Jimmy Foxx, and Lou Gehrig in succession. All of those players are now Hall of Famers. Japanese baseball fans went wild over Eiji's incredible achievement.

Eiji lost the game 1-0, but he was signed to play for Japan's first professional baseball team, the Yomiuri Giants. Other teams were created and, in 1936, Japanese pro baseball was born.

Chapter Four
Golf and Other Western Sports

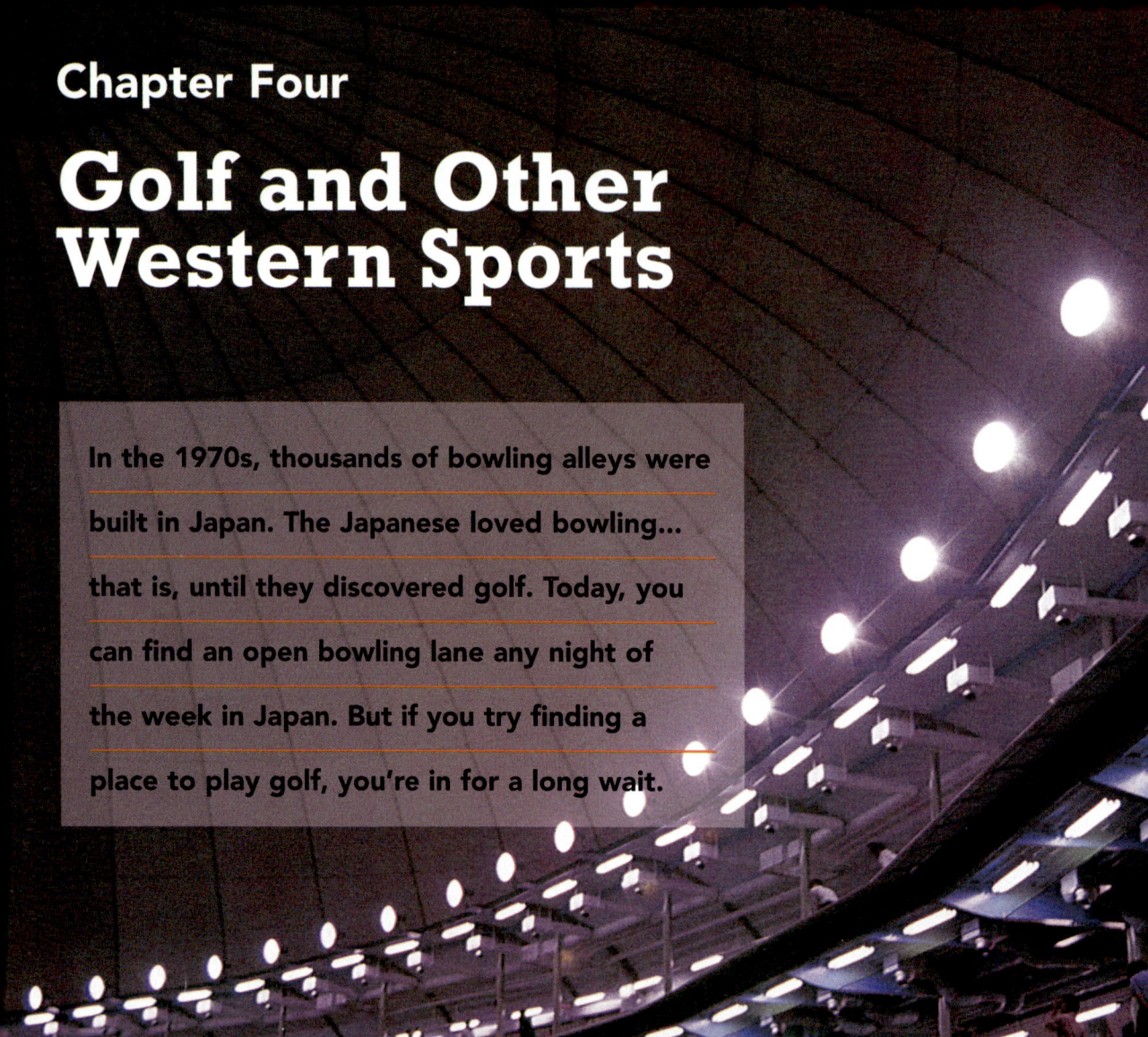

In the 1970s, thousands of bowling alleys were built in Japan. The Japanese loved bowling... that is, until they discovered golf. Today, you can find an open bowling lane any night of the week in Japan. But if you try finding a place to play golf, you're in for a long wait.

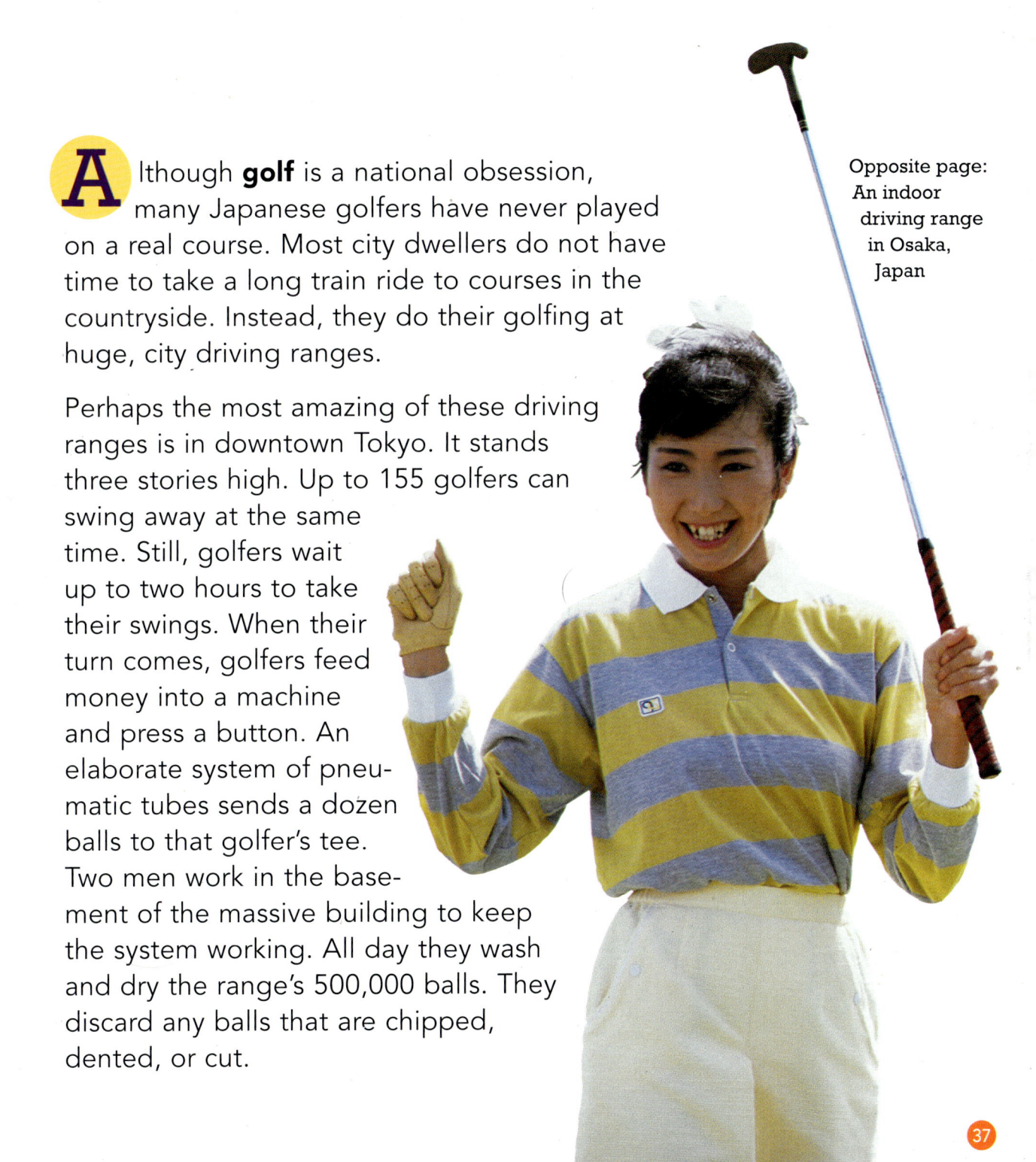

Although **golf** is a national obsession, many Japanese golfers have never played on a real course. Most city dwellers do not have time to take a long train ride to courses in the countryside. Instead, they do their golfing at huge, city driving ranges.

Perhaps the most amazing of these driving ranges is in downtown Tokyo. It stands three stories high. Up to 155 golfers can swing away at the same time. Still, golfers wait up to two hours to take their swings. When their turn comes, golfers feed money into a machine and press a button. An elaborate system of pneumatic tubes sends a dozen balls to that golfer's tee. Two men work in the basement of the massive building to keep the system working. All day they wash and dry the range's 500,000 balls. They discard any balls that are chipped, dented, or cut.

Opposite page:
An indoor driving range in Osaka, Japan

otsukiai

to socialize for
business reasons

Many Japanese golfers hate the game. But whether they like it or not, some are actually forced to play. Business people are expected to entertain clients at fancy country clubs, where golf is the main activity. This practice is called *otsukiai,* which means "socializing for business reasons." Memberships in such country clubs can cost as much as three million dollars!

Some clubs are perched high up in the mountains. It was here, in the thin air, that the odd tradition of the "oxygen bar" began. Patrons at such bars pay about one dollar to breathe a minute of pure oxygen from a special mask. The oxygen is flavored with mint, coffee, orange, or lemon. It is believed that breathing pure oxygen increases your concentration, and thus improves your golf score. Most clubs also offer golfers a hot bath and massage halfway through the course.

Many thousands of Japanese golfers take special trips each year to Hawaii specifically to try the Hawaiian courses. Others travel to Great Britain to play on the legendary courses where the game was born centuries ago.

The best a golfer can do when playing a hole is to shoot a hole-in-one. This is when the golfer tees off and puts the ball in the cup on one swing, rather than taking three, four, or more swings to reach the hole. When a Japanese player shoots a hole-in-one, he or she must hold a big party for friends and relatives. The golfer must also give fancy gifts to those who were present for the lucky shot. The caddie must be given a watch or some other valuable object to mark the occasion. Also, the golfer is expected to plant a tree on the golf course where the shot was made. Just as Japanese baseball is rich with ritual and team spirit, golf also has its own, distinctive Japanese qualities.

The beautiful setting at a country club in Ichihara, Japan

Devotion to Form

Why is Japan so obsessed with golf? Perhaps it relates to the Japanese devotion to "form." The Japanese believe there are certain ways a person should do everything. The way a person performs a task is more important than the outcome of the task. To improve at golf, your swing must be constantly adjusted. Achieving perfect "form" will lead to success. The Japanese use the same philosophy in sports, as well as in business, religion, and the arts. The ancient tea ceremony, calligraphy, and flower arranging are three activities Japanese people have practiced for many generations. The cherished quality of each is the way they are performed.

Above: Young people celebrate the new year by participating in a Tokyo calligraphy exhibition.

Right: The cherished art of flower arranging

Calligraphy

In ancient times, it was believed that a person's character could be seen in the way he or she wrote. Today, *shodo* (which means "the way of writing" and is called "calligraphy" in the West) is the most highly regarded art form in Japan. Some calligraphers copy poems or manuscripts using special letters and words called *kanji* or *kana*. Others paint scenes of mountains, oceans, and forests using only a few carefully chosen brushstrokes. Many children take part in calligraphy contests.

Calligraphers use a thick, absorbent paper called *washi*, a fast-drying black ink called *sumi*, and soft brushes called *fude* to do their beautiful work. Because of the fast-drying ink and absorbent paper, every stroke of the brush is permanent. A single mistake can destroy many hours of effort. For this reason, it takes tremendous patience and concentration to be a great calligrapher.

Flower Arranging

Many Japanese homes have special alcoves or shelves called *tokonoma* built specifically to hold seasonal arrangements of flowers. Flowers are important in Japanese culture. As part of their training to be wives, young women have traditionally been taught *kado*, "the way of flowers." The art of Japanese flower arrangement is now taught in special schools throughout the world.

The Tea Ceremony

Not long ago in Japan, young women received formal training to become "good wives." Cooking, flower arranging, and conducting a tea ceremony (left) were considered the three arts a woman must master in order to marry well. Learning to prepare and serve tea correctly was a crucial part of this training.

The tea ceremony was originally a sixteenth-century religious rite performed in monasteries. There, Buddhist monks used different types of teas as medicines and as stimulants to allow them to meditate for long periods of time. As tea took on religious significance, the ceremonies surrounding it became more and more elaborate.

Even the boiling of water for tea requires "mindfulness"— a heightened concentration on a task. The tea ceremony requires an exacting attention to form that we in the United States might find strange. The Japanese believe this makes life beautiful and enriches the spirit.

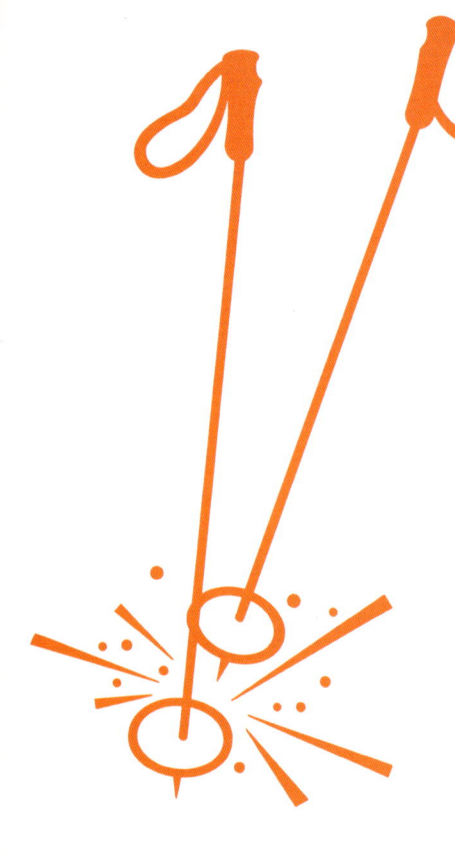

Japan's mountainous terrain makes it nearly impossible to build new golf courses. But **skiing** utilizes one of Japan's great natural features, its mountains. Snowy slopes are everywhere, and skiing has become so popular that Japan is the world's largest consumer of snow skis.

This does not mean, however, that a resident of Tokyo has an easier time finding a place to ski than finding a place to golf. Many people board special trains after work on Saturday and ride all night to ski resorts in the mountains. Once there, lines for the lift to the top of the mountain can be two hours long. After enjoying just a day on the slopes, the weekend skiers spend Sunday night riding the train back to the city. They arrive home just in time to go to work Monday morning. Even leisure can become work in Japan!

To solve such traveling problems, some indoor ski runs have been built in cities throughout Japan. One such run is made of ice that is ground up and spread over a long, sloping track. Other facilities hide snowmaking machines in the ceiling. The machines switch on periodically, to the delight of indoor skiers. Still others use a carpeted treadmill that slides beneath the rider's skis while he or she stays in place.

Indoor skiing in Sudanuma, Japan

In addition to baseball, many other Western sports are gaining popularity in Japan — such as the American sport of basketball (left) and the rough British sport of rugby (below).

Japanese pride is on display whenever Japan's athletes compete in the Olympics.

Midori Ito

The Japanese also love **Olympic** competition. They do not, however, have a great tradition of winning gold medals in the Winter or Summer Games. This may be because Japanese people tend to be small in height. Japanese mostly excel in sports where size and strength are not so important. Japanese ski-jumpers are always among the world's best, as are their speed-skaters and figure-skaters. In the Summer Olympics, Japanese long-distance runners are usually in the hunt for medals. They always do well in judo, too.

Kristi Yamaguchi

Kristi and Midori

In women's figure skating, the triple axel was once thought impossible. The jump requires a skater to leap high enough in the air to spin around three full times before landing. Also, this leaping and spinning must happen while the skater is speeding forward. But Japanese skater **Midori Ito** arrived at the 1992 Winter Olympics having landed the jump several times in competition. She was considered a favorite to win the Olympic gold medal. She felt her country was counting on her to win.

Midori Ito's main competitor was **Kristi Yamaguchi**, a Japanese-American who grew up in California. Even though Yamaguchi could not perform a triple axel, she dazzled the Olympic judges with a graceful, enchanting performance. When the final scores were tallied, Kristi won the gold medal for first place, and Midori won the second-place silver medal. Japan was proud of Midori Ito, and Yamaguchi became one of the most famous and popular Japanese-Americans ever. She even had her picture on a Wheaties box!

Chapter Five
Games Kids Play

When Japanese children must decide who will bat first in baseball, or who is "it" for hide-and-seek, they do the same thing most American kids do: they play *jan*, *ken*, *po*. We call the game "rock, paper, scissors."

October 10 is a "national sports day" in Japan. In celebration, schools hold *undokai*—what we might call a "field day." The games played at undokai emphasize teamwork over individual victories. In one game, called **tama-ire,** two teams try to toss colored sponge balls into a bucket at the top of a pole. When the teacher blows a whistle to stop play, the balls are counted. The team that has tossed the most balls into the bucket wins. There is, of course, no way to know which individual player got the most balls in the bucket. So all the members of the winning team share the credit equally. This emphasis on teamwork over individual winning or losing is very important to the Japanese. Children are taught constantly that they must be part of a team to be successful and happy.

Above: Kids and adults play *tama-ire.*

Opposite page: *Jan, ken, po* — the Japanese version of "rock, paper, scissors."

The Japanese game of *go* is popular in both its traditional form (above), and its modern Internet version (below).

Japanese kids also play a game called **go**. Go is a Japanese board game that is played all over the world. "Go" means "five" in Japanese. The game is a bit like tic-tac-toe played on a bigger board. Two players take turns placing either black or white tokens on a checkerboard. The object is to place five of your tokens in a row. In a variation called "bean go," you try instead to surround your opponent's tokens with yours.

Not only children play go. Some people play every day and take the game quite seriously. They consider the game a "way of life." Today, computer go matches up opponents in foreign countries using the Internet!

Kids, especially boys, love to catch **bugs**. Many Japanese children keep crickets as pets. Traditionally, the Japanese love to hear the cricket's song, and crickets are considered good luck. More exciting for boys are the *kabuto mushi*, or "helmet beetles," that emerge from the ground in early summer. These insects are prized for their resemblance to a sort of robot samurai warrior. They appear to be wearing an elaborate helmet and have nasty pincers. They are found quite easily. Once a child captures one, they groom the beetle for battles. It is common to find a circle of young kids watching a pair of tiny beetle warriors fight it out.

kabuto mushi

helmet beetles

Many Japanese children collect beetles as pets.

This happy girl examines her collection of dolls on the day of the annual Japanese Doll Festival. These dolls are for display only, and are not meant to be played with.

omocho

honorable object to play with

Japanese kids love many of the same new **toys** American kids love. In fact, the idea of "changing" toys (such as Transformers) was invented in Japan. These are action figures that, with a few twists and turns, change into robots, monsters, airplanes, or tanks.

Some toys in Japan have religious significance. These are called *omocho*, which means "honorable object to play with." At Shinto shrines, one can purchase toy horses, *daruma* dolls, and toy lions. Clay or papier-mâché dogs called *inu hariko* are believed to protect children from evil spirits that might make them sick.

Each year on March 3, a festival called *hina matsuri* takes place. Beautiful sets of brightly painted dolls are displayed in homes throughout Japan. And during the New Year's Festival, girls play a game called *hanetsuki*. The game is much like badminton played with beautifully decorated paddles and shuttlecocks.

Children also play with tops, or *koma*. *Kendama* is what Japanese kids call the ball-in-cup game that has frustrated people everywhere for centuries. A wooden cup sits atop a stick, to which is attached a ball on a string. The object is to flip the ball on the string into the cup.

Pachinko began as a toy but has become an obsession for some Japanese. Seventy percent of all Japanese men and 30 percent of women play regularly. A pachinko machine is a little like a pinball machine. Players launch steel balls, which bounce and fall down a vertical maze. Pachinko's tinkling balls and ringing bells have an almost hypnotic effect on many players. Some people sit in pachinko parlors (below) for hours at a time. The game involves a little skill and a lot of luck. Winners can trade in steel balls for chocolate, canned food, and other prizes. There are even professional pachinko players and a magazine devoted to the game.

Chapter Six

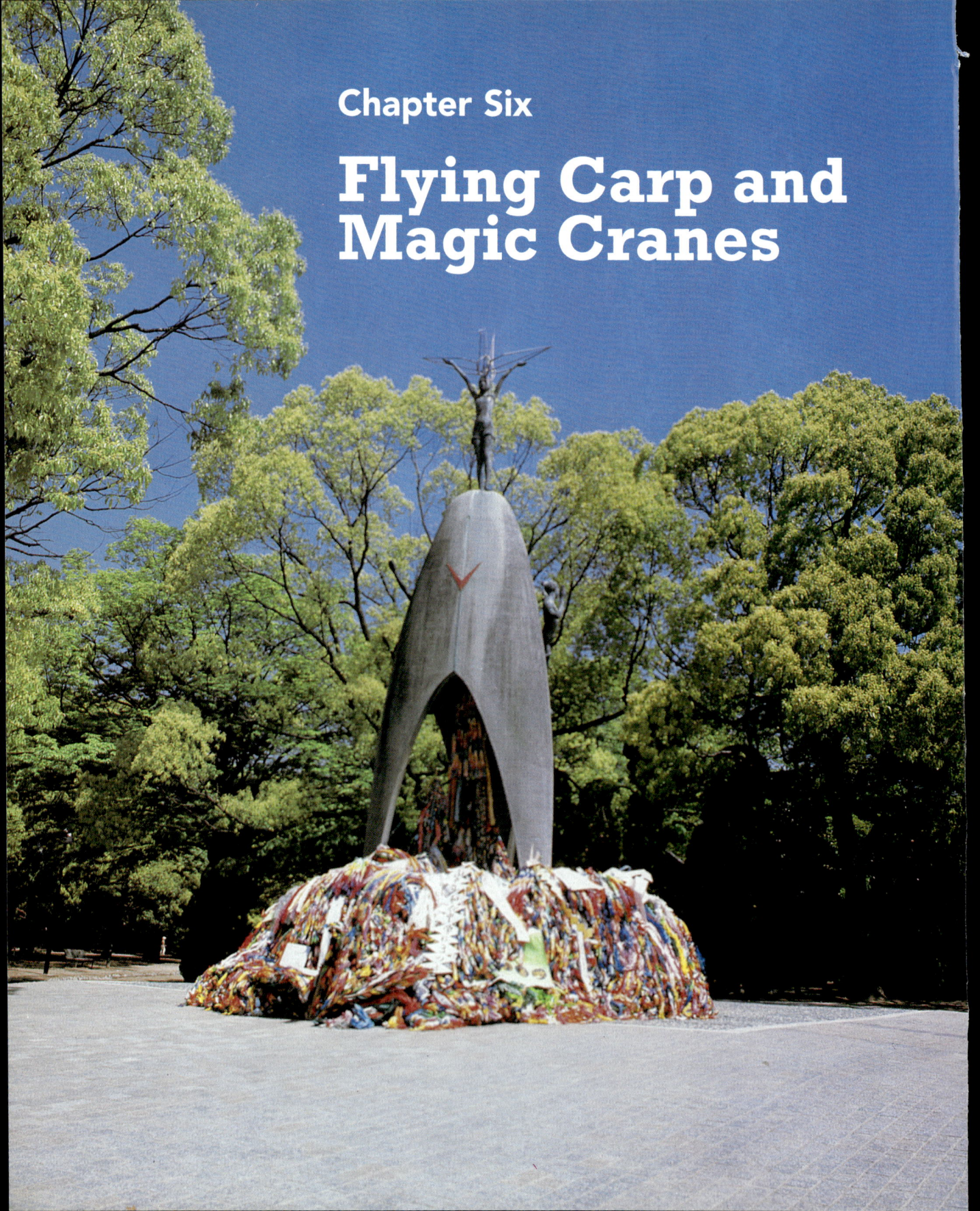

Flying Carp and Magic Cranes

A Buddhist priest brought the art of paper-making to Japan from China in about A.D. 538. Monks and priests began making a thick, fibrous kind of paper called *washi*. It became a tradition on ceremonial occasions to fold this paper into various animal shapes and abstract designs. Paper-folding, called **origami** in Japan, is one of Japan's oldest art forms.

An Origami Memorial

In August 1945, the United States brought World War II to a shocking end when it dropped two atomic bombs on the Japanese cities of Hiroshima and Nagasaki. The bombs unleashed incredible destruction, and the intense radiation they emitted caused illnesses in people for years. Sadako Sasaki was a schoolgirl who survived the bombing of Hiroshima, but she eventually developed the deadly disease leukemia. Once she learned she was ill, Sadako began folding origami cranes. She believed that if she could fold one thousand cranes she would live. Sadly, she died after folding 964 cranes. Her friends and classmates folded the rest for her and placed them in Hiroshima's Peace Park (opposite page). The park memorializes all those who died as a result of the atomic bomb. Schoolchildren still leave thousands of origami cranes there to honor the dead.

About Origami Paper

For origami, the only material you need is paper. It's best to use a paper that will fold easily. Thin paper (such as tissue) or very thick paper (such as cardboard or construction paper) will not work well for most origami projects. Common computer or photocopy paper will work well. If you want to recycle paper, you can use pages from discarded magazines.

Art supply stores carry many beautiful types of origami paper. You can also make your own origami paper by decorating a sheet of white or colored paper. Use magic markers to draw colorful patterns of lines, stars, or flowers on one side of the paper.

For most origami projects, start with a square piece of paper. For a small origami figure, cut your paper to four inches by four inches. For a larger figure, use a six-by-six-inch square of paper. When you're just starting out with origami, it's best not to use paper that is much smaller or larger than these sizes.

How Do I Play?

The word *origami* comes from the Japanese terms *ori*, which means "folded," and *kami*, which means "paper." You can make simple origami figures with only a few folds of paper, or you can spend hours making a complex figure involving hundreds of folds. There is no limit to the different kinds of figures that you can make. All kinds of animals are available to the origami-maker—from simple fish and birds to more complex spiders and dinosaurs. You can also make human figures, flowers, airplanes, ships, hats, and more just by folding paper. On the opposite page are instructions on how to make one of the easiest origami figures—a dog.

1. Cut out a square of paper that measures four inches by four inches.

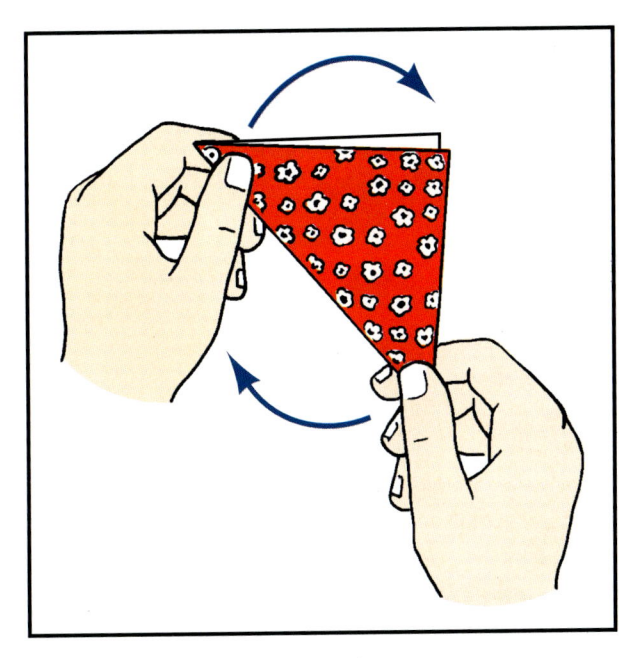

2. Fold the paper diagonally to make a triangle. Turn the triangle upside down.

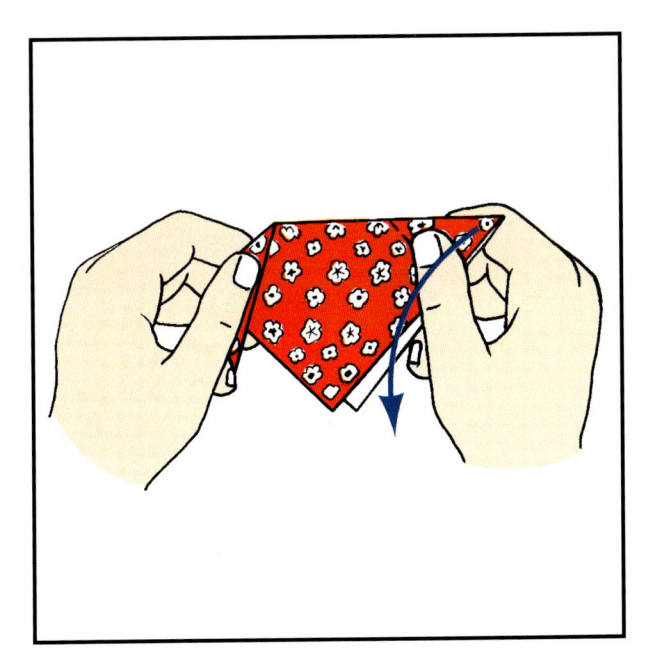

3. Fold down the top corners to make your origami dog's "ears."

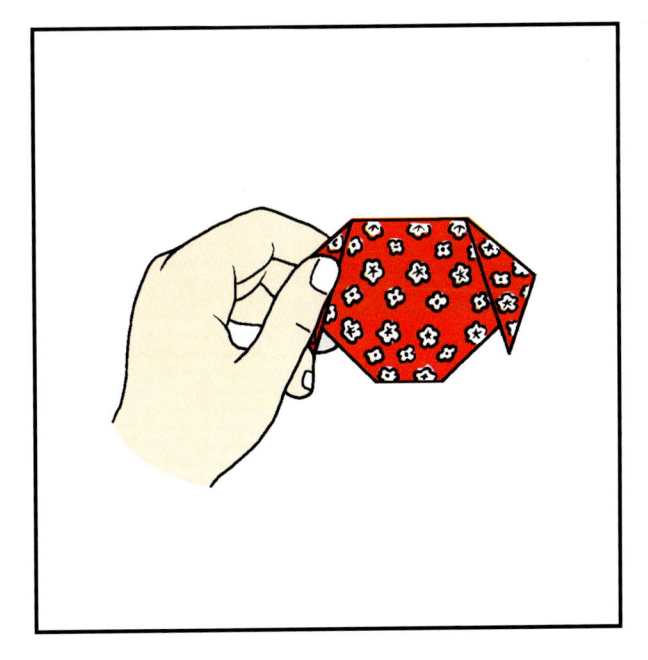

4. Fold up the bottom corner to make the dog's "mouth."

55

Thousands of origami cranes are placed at the base of the Hiroshima memorial.

The most common and important shape in origami is *tsuru*, the bird we call the "crane." Cranes are traditional symbols of good luck. An ancient Japanese legend says that to fold one thousand cranes will lead to a long life filled with good fortune. A similar legend states that if you fold and string together a thousand cranes, the gods will grant you a single wish.

Building and flying **kites** is another popular activity in Japan. Japanese kites are often elaborate. They have bamboo frames and are brightly painted. They become warriors, birds, huge insects, or brightly patterned shapes in the sky. There are four basic shapes for kites: rectangular, polygonal, windbag, or *kimono*.

Kites, like origami, were introduced by Buddhist priests in the tenth century. People originally flew kites to ask divine spirits for a good rice harvest, healthy children, and peace. If these wishes were granted, other kites were flown to say "thank you" to the friendly spirits. Still other kites flew above a monastery or village to purify the ground below and chase away evil spirits.

It takes many people to launch this huge kite in a park at Sagamihara, Japan.

A Japanese kite

The military soon began using kites to send messages and signals to distant soldiers.

By the 1600s, wealthy merchants and lords began to fly kites for fun. Today, huge kite tournaments are held in Japan. Specially fitted kites engage in airborne battles. The string on such kites is partially covered with particles of glass. This allows one kite to slice through the string of another, sending the loser spiraling to earth. Prizes are also awarded to the most beautiful and elaborate kites.

On May 5 every year, kites in the shape of **carp** are hung on bamboo poles outside family homes. A big, black carp represents the father. A smaller red carp is the mother. A blue carp is hung for each child in the home. The Japanese call this day *kodomo-no-hi*, or Children's Day. Carp are symbols of courage and perseverance because they swim upstream, against the current.

Flying carp outside a Japanese home

Glossary

apprentice
a person learning a profession or skill from a more experienced person

akido
martial art that emphasizes graceful movement to escape an attacker

basho
sumo wrestling competitions that determine Japan's grand champion

bushido
Japanese word meaning "the way of the warrior," a code of honor invented by samurai warriors

driving range
a long field where golfers practice by swinging at one ball after another while standing in the same spot

emperor
the traditional leader of Japan whose role is now only ceremonial

feudal (or feudalism)
ancient system of government in which wealthy lords controlled large areas of land and charged people to farm and live there

feudal lords
powerful people in ancient times who owned large pieces of land and many servants

form
a way of doing something that is determined by rules of tradition or custom

gyoj
the referee in a sumo wrestling match

go
Japanese board game using colored markers and a checkerboard

hemp
a plant used to make rope or twine

jan, ken, go
Japanese version of "rock, paper, scissors"

judo
martial art in which opponents attempt to throw each other to the ground

jujitsu
another word for judo

kami
divine spirits of the Shinto religion that help ensure human happiness and success

karate
martial art in which opponents use kicks and jabs to strike each other's weakest points

kata
Japanese word for "form," meaning the correct way of performing an activity

kendo
martial art of sword fighting

kyudo
a Japanese form of archery

martial arts
several combat skills invented by samurai and now practiced as sports; includes karate, judo, akido, and others

medieval
the Middle Ages (from about A.D. 500 to about 1500)

meditation
mental exercise in which a person strives to achieve very deep concentration; focusing the mind on itself

mindfulness
extreme concentration in which a person is very aware of all aspects of the activity he or she is performing

origami
Japanese art of folding paper

purify
to remove anything unclean (or unholy) from a place or object

resin
sticky substance usually made from tree sap; used to improve an athlete's grip on a ball, bowstring, or other piece of equipment

rigorous
strict, severe, or difficult

sake
Japanese wine made out of fermented rice

samurai
warrior of the feudal era in Japan

Shinto
ancient Japanese religion

shodo
Japanese term for "calligraphy," or the art of writing

shogun
warrior who ruled in ancient Japan

sumotori
professional sumo wrestler

sushi
a popular Japanese way of preparing fish, which is often served raw

teppo
heavy wooden pole used in training by sumo wrestlers

wa
Japanese term meaning "group harmony"; achieved when a group of people work together toward a common goal, without jealousy or selfishness

washi
a thick, handmade paper used in calligraphy and origami

yokozuna
Japanese word meaning "grand champion"; the highest rank of a sumo wrestler

Index

(**Boldface** page numbers indicate illustrations.)

Aaron, Henry ("Hank"), 33
Akebono (Chad Rowan), **19**
akido, 25, 27
archery, 26–27

Baltimore Orioles, 30
baseball, 7, **9**, 28–35, **28, 30, 31, 32, 33, 34, 35**
basketball, 7, **43**
bowling, 36
Buddhism, 8
bug collecting, 49, **49**
bullet train, **6**
bushido, 21, 22, 27, 29

Calligraphy, 40, **40,** 41
carp, 59, **59**

Central League, 34
cheerleaders, 34–35, **34**
China, 22, 53
Christianity, 8
Cracker Jack, 34

Dolls, 50, **50**

Emperor's Cup, 11

Flower arranging, 40, **40,** 41
football, 7
Foxx, Jimmy, 35

Gehrig, Lou, 35
Gehringer, Charlie, 35
Germany, 8
go, 48, **48**
golf, 7, 36–40, **36, 37, 39**
Great Britain, 38

Hanetsuki, 51
Hawaii, 38
Hiroshima Carp, 34
Hiroshima, Japan, 53
Hiroshima Peace Park, **52,** 53, **56**
Hokkaido, Japan, 8
Honshu, Japan, 8

Internet, 48
Ito, Midori, 45, **45**

Jan, ken, po, 46, **46**
Japan
geography of, 8
government of, 8
and education, 5
and "form," 22, 40–41
history of, 8
map of, 9
and play, 5–7
and work ethic, 4–7
Japanese World Series, 35
judo, 6, 24, **24,** 25, **25,** 27, 45
jujitsu, 25

Karate, 22–23, **22**, **23**, 27
  kendama, 51
  kendo, 26, **26**, 27
  kites, 57–59, **57**, **58**, **59**
  kyudo, 26, 27, **27**
  Kyushu, Japan, 8

Little League, **30**, **32**

Martial arts, 20–27, **20, 21, 22, 23, 24, 25, 26, 27**
  Mutshuhito, 8

Nagasaki, Japan, 53
  ninja, 21
  Nippon Ham-Fighters, 35

Oh, Sadahara, **28**, 33, **33**
  Okinawa, 22
  Olympic Games, 24, **24**
  origami, 53–56, **52, 53, 54, 55, 56,** 57
  oxygen bars, 38

Pachinko, 51, **51**
  Pacific League, 34
  Pacific Ocean, 8

Ripken Jr., Cal, 30
  rock, paper, scissors, 46
  Rowan, Chad. *See* Akebono
  rugby, **43**
  running, 45
  Ruth, Babe, 35

Sagamihara, Japan, 57
  sake, 34
  samurai, 20–21, 26–27
  San Francisco Giants, 29
  Sasaki, Sadako, 53
  Sawamura, Eija, 35
  Shikoku, Japan, 8
  Shinto, 8, 12, 14, 50
  skiing, 42, **42**
  Smith, Reggie, 29
  sumo wrestling, 6–7, 10–19, **10, 11, 12, 13, 14, 15, 16, 17, 18, 19**
  Super Bowl, 11
  sushi, 34

Tama-ire, 47, **47**
  tea ceremony, 40, 41, **41**
  Tokyo Dome, **9**
  Tokyo, Japan, 8, 34, 37
  toys, 50

United States (and Americans), 8, 11, 24, 28, 29, 30, 33, 38, 41, 45, 53
  University of Tokyo, 33

Wheaties, 45
  Wilson, Horace, 33
  World War II, 8, 24, 53

Yabusame, **20, 21**
  Yamaguchi, Kristi, 45, **45**
  Yomiuri Giants, 29, 35

Photo Credits

Cover ©Michael S. Yamashita; 1 (top left and right), Reuters/Bettmann; 1 (bottom), 2–3, 4, ©Cameramann International, Ltd.; 5, ©Charles Gupton/Tony Stone Images; 6, Tony Stone Images; 7, ©Cameramann International, Ltd.; 9, ©Charles Gupton/Tony Stone Images; 10, 11, ©Cameramann International, Ltd.; 12 (left), ©C. Ursillo/H. Armstrong Roberts; 12 (right), ©Chris Cole/Tony Stone Images; 13, Reuters/Bettmann; 14 (top and bottom), The Bettmann Archive; 15, ©Robert Holmes/Tony Stone Images; 16, 17, ©Michael S. Yamashita; 18, ©Cameramann International, Ltd.; 19, Reuters/Bettmann; 20, ©Jack G. Beasley/Uniphoto Press/Photri; 21, ©Steve Vidler/SuperStock International, Inc.; 22, Reuters/Bettmann; 23 (two photos), ©Michael S. Yamashita; 24, Reuters/Bettmann; 25, The Bettmann Archive; 26, ©Cameramann International, Ltd.; 27, ©Orion Press/Photri; 28, UPI/Bettmann; 30, ©Cameramann International, Ltd.; 31, Reuters/Bettmann; 32, ©Orion Press/Photri; 33, AP/Wide World Photos; 34 (left), ©Cameramann International, Ltd.; 34 (right), ©Michael S. Yamashita; 35, Reuters/Bettmann; 36, ©Michael S. Yamashita; 37, ©Orion Press/Photri; 39, ©Michael S. Yamashita; 40 (two photos), ©Cameramann International, Ltd.; 41, ©Orion Press/Photri; 42, AP/Wide World Photos; 43 (bottom), ©Michael S. Yamashita; 43 (top), ©Orion Press/Photri; 44, ©Kurt Scholz/SuperStock International, Inc.; 45 (top), Reuters/Bettmann; 45 (bottom), AP/Wide World Photos; 46, ©Orion Press/Photri; 47, ©Tom Wagner/Odyssey/Chicago; 48 (bottom), Reuters/Bettmann; 48 (top), 49, ©Orion Press/Photri; 50, ©Bob & Ira Spring; 51, Reuters/Bettmann; 52, 53, 54, ©Orion Press/Photri; 56, 57, 58, 59, ©Orion Press/Photri

About the Author

Philip Brooks grew up near Chicago and now lives in Columbus, Ohio, with his wife, Balinda Craig-Quijada. He attended the University of Iowa Writers' Workshop, where he received an M.F.A. in fiction writing. His stories have appeared in a number of literary magazines, and he has written several books for children. He is the author of *Michael Jordan: Beyond Air* and *Dikembe Mutombo: Mount Mutombo* (Children's Press), and the Franklin Watts First Books *Georgia O'Keeffe* and *Mary Cassatt*.